DATE DUE

SBH	OCT 21		
FS 3	DEC 16		
LS 8	FEB 24		
VM E	MAR 22		
PF 4	APR 20		
LR 4	OCT 23		

DEMCO 38-297

Published by Creative Education
123 South Broad Street, Mankato, Minnesota 56001
Creative Education is an imprint of The Creative Company

Designed by Stephanie Blumenthal
Production Design by Patricia Bickner Linder

Photographs by: AP/Wide World, Corbis-Bettmann, Earth Images,
FPG International, International Stock, and Tom Stack & Associates

Library of Congress Cataloging-in-Publication Data

Richardson, Adele, 1966–
Mexico / by Adele Richardson
p. cm. — (Let's Investigate)
Includes glossary.
Summary: Introduces the geography, daily life, history, culture,
and natural resources of Mexico
ISBN 0-88682-984-4
1. Mexico—Juvenile literature. [1. Mexico.]
I. Title. II. Series: Let's Investigate (Mankato, Minn.)
F1208.5.R5   1999
972—dc21   97-14261

First edition

2 4 6 8 9 7 5 3 1

MEXICO

ADELE RICHARDSON

Creative Education

MEXICO
FACT

When Mexicans say "Mexico," they actually mean Mexico City. When talking about the country they say "the republic."

Mayan relief *sculpture* of a warrior

Mexican people still cherish traditions that have been around for thousands of years. Yet, at the same time, their country offers the world many valuable resources. Mexicans have successfully combined the old and the new, making their country an important part of our world.

LAND AND CLIMATE

Mexico is the southern-most country in North America. To the north, it borders the United States. This border is 1,429 miles (2,300 km) long. To the south, it touches the countries of Guatemala and Belize. A trip through Mexico from north to south would take a person across 1,914 miles (3,080 km) of beautiful **landscape.**

The Yucatán Peninsula

MEXICO
BORDER

The river Rio Bravo (called the Rio Grande in the United States) forms more than 1,000 miles (1,610 km) of the border between Mexico and the United States.

5

MEXICO

TREES

Twenty percent of the land in Mexico is covered with forests.

MEXICO

FACT

Mexico City is the most populated city in the world; more than 20 million people live there.

Right, Temple of the Cross (left) and Temple of the Sun at Palenque

Mexico's landscape has great variety. It is filled with jungles, deserts, and many beaches. The three mountain ranges that run north and south through the country are named Sierra Madre ("sierra" means mountain range). Mexico's highest mountain is Pico de Orizaba. It towers over the country at 18,410 feet (5,610 m). This mountain is actually a volcano. It is so high that the temperature at its peak stays below freezing all year long, making it the coldest place in the country.

exico has two **peninsulas.** The Yucatán Peninsula is on the eastern side of the country and is filled with many jungles. The Baja California Peninsula is on the west coast. It is one of the world's longest peninsulas at nearly 800 miles (1,288 km) long. This peninsula is home to many mountains and dry deserts.

The smallest breed of dog in the world, the Chihuahua, came from Mexico.

7

Below, carving of the ancient Mexican god Quetzalcoatl

Silk City, U.S.A.

Using raw silk imported from Asia, silk manufacturing grew in the eastern United States after 1865, when tariffs, or taxes, on goods imported from Europe were raised. At this time, there was a high demand for silk in the **fashion industry**. By 1880, silk mills in Paterson, New Jersey, were producing almost half of America's silk. Paterson was built on the Passaic River, which provided power for the town's silk mills and many other types of mills. Paterson was also close to New York, which was where raw silk imported from China, Japan, and Italy entered the United States. Skilled silk workers immigrated to Paterson from Italy, France, Germany, and England to work in the mills.

Workers march in New York City in support of the Patterson silk strike of 1913.

Striking Silk Workers

For ten hours a day, five and a half days a week, workers toiled in the silk mills in Paterson, New Jersey. Some of the factories were dyeing mills, where workers dyed silk thread and fabric in large vats of hot water and chemicals. Other mills were weaving mills, where workers used looms to weave silk cloth and ribbon. In 1911, silk mill owners tried to change their work system so that weavers ran four looms at a time, instead of two. Fearing that this would create a loss in jobs and quality of woven cloth, 800 silk weavers went on strike in January 1913. Soon after, they were joined by workers from 300 other types of mills in the town. The strike ended seven months later, by which time silk mill owners had lost an estimated $10 million in profits because of the strikes.

Young Textile Workers

Today, silk is made in many Asian countries. In some countries, raising silkworms is done by families in villages. Often, children are expected to help their families care for the worms.

Children in the Mills

Child labor was historically used in silk and other textile mills in England and the United States. Children were hired by mill owners because they worked for lower wages and were less likely to strike. In England, children were purchased from orphanages and workhouses and forced to work in textile mills. Mill owners fed and clothed the young workers, who were referred to as "apprentices" but did not pay them wages and, in some cases, refused to let them leave the mills. Children also worked long hours and performed dangerous jobs involving machinery. Throughout the 1800s, laws were passed in England and in the United States to try to restrict child labor in textile mills.

Teenage boys reel silk at the New Jersey Worsted Spinning Company. Children were employed to work in silk mills in Paterson, New Jersey, and in other silk mills in North America and Europe.

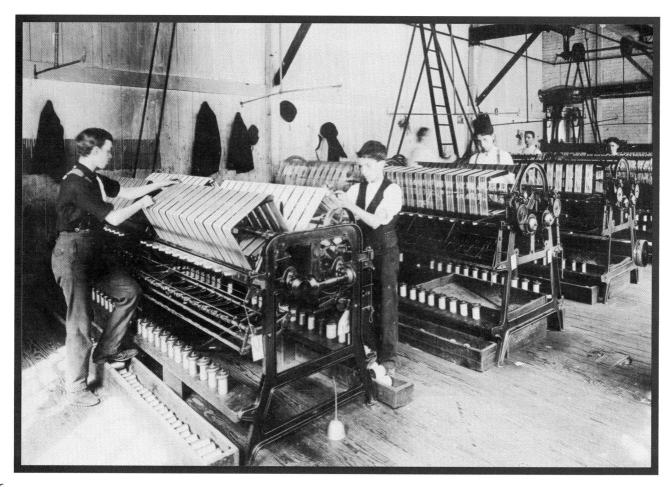

(above) In 2005, hundreds of child laborers were rescued in Bombay, India, and returned to their homes. The children were working in factories that manufacture leather, steel, and silk embroidered goods.

India's Child Workers

Human rights organizations report that children work in India's silk factories today. Children under the age of 14 are said to work as many as 84 hours per week making silk thread. They do jobs such as washing the silk in steamy water to loosen the cocoons. According to some reports, the children are badly burned from their work and some are beaten by their employers. The children work under a system called bonded labor, which means that their parents have borrowed money from a factory owner and the children have to work until the debt is repaid. India's government is working to end bonded child labor in its silk factories.

(right) A young worker embroiders with silk thread in a Chinese factory.

Silk Uses

The main use of silk today is in the fashion industry. Many items of clothing are made out of silk, including shirts, dresses, and pants. Items made only from natural silk are more expensive to buy than goods made of silk blended, or combined, with other natural fabrics, such as cotton, or with synthetic materials.

Synthetic Silk

Synthetic silk is fabric made from human-made fibers. Alchemists, or early chemists, tried to make silk from other materials in the Middle Ages. Rayon and nylon are two types of synthetic fabrics available today that are similar to silk in strength and **luster**, and can be used in place of natural silk. Rayon was invented in the early 1900s by Count Hillarie de Chardonnet, a scientist who worked with Louis Pasteur to solve France's silkworm problems. Nylon, made from petroleum, was invented by a chemical company called DuPont in the 1930s. Nylon was invented by Wallace Carothers, the scientist who also helped develop synthetic rubber. In 1929, nylon was introduced to the public at the New York World's Fair as the material used to make women's stockings. Nylon stockings were an instant success because they were much cheaper to buy than those made of silk.

(left) This evening gown is made of white silk.

(right) Silk-screen printing, or serigraphy, is a method of printing designs by squeegying paint or ink over a silk screen.

Silk Foods

In some Asian countries, silkworm pupae are eaten. Silkworm pupae are a source of protein. They are sold preserved in tin cans and are fried with spices before being eaten. In the past, silkworm pupae were eaten in villages in China during times of famine. Today, silkworm pupae are sold in restaurants. In Japan, waste silk has also been ground into a fine powder and made into noodles and candy.

(above) The first parachutes were made of silk in the 1700s. There was a boom in silk parachute manufacturing during World War I. Parachutes continued to be made from silk until synthetic fibers were developed during World War II.

Silk in Medicine

Silk is made out of protein. Animals and humans both need protein to be healthy. This makes silk good for use in medicine. Silk is made into artificial tendons and ligaments. Tendons are **tissues** inside the human body that connect muscles and bones, and ligaments are tissues that connect bones to bones. Silk has long been used to make sutures, or stitches used to sew up wounds in the skin. Sutures made from silk are specially manufactured.

(above) **Ppeondaegi***, or boiled silkworm pupae, is a popular treat sold by street vendors in Korea.*

29

The Future of Silk

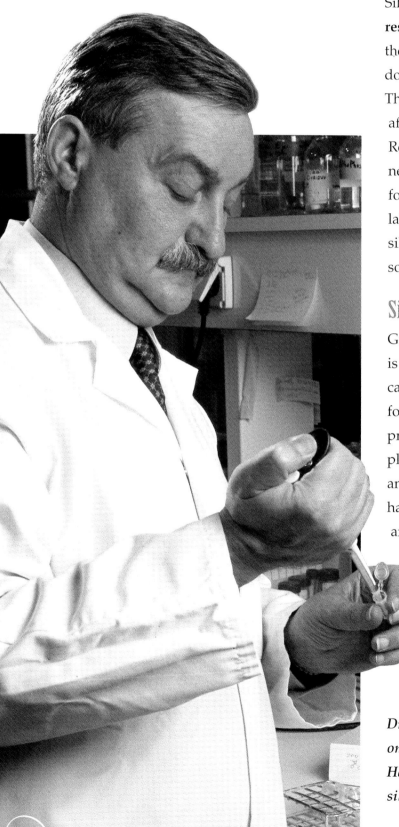

Silk is a natural fiber that is a **renewable resource**, which means that, with proper care, the supply of silk will not run out. Scientists are doing research to find new ways of using silk. They also try to breed silkworms that will not be affected by diseases and temperature changes. Research is also being made into developing new kinds of silkworms that will eat other foods besides mulberry leaves. In some laboratories, scientists are developing silkworms that produce naturally colored silks, so there will be no need to dye the threads.

Silk and the Environment

Growing mulberry trees to feed the silkworms is good for the environment because the trees can grow in soil that is too poor to grow other food crops. Like all trees, mulberry trees help protect against soil erosion, or keep the soil in place so that it is not washed away by the wind and rain. Some people argue that silk making harms the environment because so much water and chemicals are used in manufacturing. Water is used to boil the cocoons and to degum, or wash the sericin from, the filament. Almost one ton of water is used to make one ton of raw silk.

Dr. Gerard Chavancy is a French scientist and one of the world's leading silkworm experts. Here, Dr. Chavancy performs experiments on silkworms in his laboratory.

Animal Rights

Some people argue that silk production is cruel to silkworms because they are killed before they live out their entire life cycle. Silkworms have been domesticated for so long that scientists believe the moths could no longer survive in the wild without human help. For many years, silkworms that were not healthy or did not create the best silk were killed before they could breed. As well, only moths with small, weak wings were allowed to breed. This was so that the moths did not fly off to lay their eggs somewhere else, where farmers could not harvest the cocoons. Today, silkworm moths can barely fly at all. The silkworms' legs have also become very weak over the years because they no longer have to walk to find food.

(above) "Peace Silk" is a method of producing silk without killing the silkworm moth. The moths are allowed to emerge naturally from the cocoon. The broken silk fibers are then spun like other cloth fibers.

Research is being done into uses for the waste pupae. It may one day be made into oil.

Glossary

archaeologist A person who studies ancient cultures

Arab A person from present-day Saudi Arabia

bred Joined together to create offspring

colonization The period in which a country imposes its rule over another and sends settlers to live there

commercial For a profit

demand The amount wanted by buyers

dissolve To cause to fade away

domesticate To take from the wild and change the behavior of

dynasty A ruling family

East A term that refers to all the countries of Asia

fashion industry The businesses involved in designing and manufacturing clothing

fiber A thin strand

human rights organization A group of people who investigate and make others aware of the rights of people living in certain areas

import To buy in from another country

incubator An artifically heated container for hatching eggs

Islam The religion based on the teachings of the prophet Muhammad

luster Brightness, or how much light is reflected off an object

mold A fungus that grows on damp things

nomadic Moving from place to place

oasis An area in a desert that has water and vegetation

patent Legal rights as the inventor of something

predator An animal that hunts another

processed Changed from its original form and made into something else

Protestant A branch of Christianity that split from the Roman Catholic Church in the 1500s

renewable resource A resource is something found in nature that people use, such as wood, water, and oil. Renewable resources can be replenished by nature

sumptuary laws Laws passed to restrict the kinds of clothing worn by people of different social classes, or rank

tissue Groups of cells that perform a similar function

tropical Regions of the world that receive the most sunlight just north and south of the equator

warp The lengthwise yarn on a loom

weft The widthwise yarn on a loom

West A term used to describe the cultures of Europe and North America

Index

child labor 26-27

cottage industry 7, 14

dyeing 5, 12, 13, 21, 25, 30

Jacquard, Joseph-Marie 23

larvae 4, 8, 9, 10, 11, 13, 14

Lombe, John and Thomas 22

looms 12, 23, 25

mulberry trees 8, 9, 10, 13, 14, 19, 24, 30

Pasteur, Louis 23, 28

pupae 8, 9, 11, 13, 29, 31

raw silk 6, 20, 25, 30

reeling 12, 14

sericulture 4, 6, 7, 10, 14, 15, 16, 19, 23, 24, 26, 31

silk guilds 21

silk mills 22, 25, 26

synthetic silk 5, 28

throwing 4, 12, 14,

22, 31

trade 4, 16-19, 20

uses for 5, 6, 15, 20, 23, 24, 25, 28-29, 30

weaving 4, 12, 13, 14, 15, 20, 21, 22, 23, 25

wild silk 13, 19

DONALDSON WAY SCHOOL
430 DONALDSON WAY
AMERICAN CANYON, CA
94503